Great
Hispanics
of Our Time™

Jaime Escalante: Inspiring Educator

Maritza Romero

The Rosen Publishing Group's
PowerKids Press™
New York

Published in 1997 by The Rosen Publishing Group, Inc.
29 East 21st Street, New York, NY 10010

First Edition

Book Design: Danielle Primiceri

Photo Credits: Cover and p. 7 © George Rose/Gamma-Liaison; p. 4 © Cardoni/Liaison International; p. 9 © Bill Losh/FPG International; p. 11 © Skjold Photographs; pp. 12, 16 © AP/Wide World Photos; p. 15 © Al Michaud/FPG International; p. 19 © Gamma-Liaison; p. 20 © Diana Walker/Gamma Liaison.

Romero, Maritza.
    Jaime Escalante : inspiring educator / Maritza Romero.
       p.   cm. — (Great Hispanics of our time)
    Summary: The story of the Bolivian-born teacher who immigrated to the United States where he has become successful in motivating his students to excel in science and math.
    ISBN 0-8239-5085-9
    1. Escalante, Jaime—Juvenile literature. 2. Mathematics teachers—California—Biography—Juvenile literature. 3. Hispanic American mathematics teachers—California—Biography—Juvenile literature. [1. Escalante, Jaime. 2. Teachers. 3. Hispanic Americans—Biography.] I. Title. II. Series.
GA29.E73R66 1997
510'.92—dc21
                                          97-11603
                                               CIP
                                             AC

Contents

Word Games

Jaime Escalante was born on December 31, 1930 in La Paz, Bolivia, a country in South America. His parents were both teachers. He spent a lot of time with his grandfather, who had also been a teacher. Jaime's grandfather played word games with him. He asked him to spell word after word. Most of the time, Jaime got the answers right. His mother also taught him lessons. She told him, "If I teach you something, or make you remember something, you'll have it forever."

◀ Jaime Escalante was born and raised in La Paz, Bolivia.

A Good Talker

As a student, Jaime was known for many things. He was very good at math. He loved to figure things out. He often looked ahead in his math book to see what he would be learning next in class. He was also good at sports such as soccer, basketball, and hand-ball, which was his favorite.

Jaime also liked to fight. He often got into trouble at school because he would get into fights with other boys. But he was good at talking to people. He could talk his way out of trouble most of the time.

As a teacher, Jaime used the communication skills he had learned as a child. ▶

A Search for Information

Jaime loved to learn new things. He began to **experiment** (ex-PEER-ih-ment) to see how things worked. But sometimes he got into trouble with his experiments. When he was a teenager, he built wooden cars to push down the hilly streets in his neighborhood. One time he pushed his little sister, Bertha, in one of his cars and she fell through an open manhole!

Jaime liked to experiment with **electricity** (el-ek-TRIH-sih-tee) to see what it could do. He once set a small electrical fire. It burned his older sister Olimpia's foot, but she was okay.

◀ Like this girl, Jaime liked to experiment and learn new things, especially in science.

Learning While Doing

Jaime wanted to be an **electrical engineer** (ee-LEK-trih-kul en-jin-EER), but his family didn't have enough money to send him to college to study that. So he decided to try teaching instead. While he was learning to be a teacher, he was given the chance to teach a high school **physics** (FIZ-iks) class. He was only 21 years old and he hadn't had any classes on how to teach. So he learned how to teach by actually teaching. If something didn't work, he tried a new way of teaching.

Most teachers go to school to learn how to teach. ▶
Jaime learned how to teach by doing it.

The Cat

To earn money for his family, Jaime taught at three different schools before he even finished college. He was soon known all over Bolivia as an excellent teacher. His students called him "the Cat" because he snuck up on them in class to ask them whether they knew the answers to math problems. They were afraid of him. But Jaime's **strategy** (STRA-tuh-jee) worked. His students remembered what he told them. And they did well. He finished college in 1954 and began teaching high school math and physics. He also married a teacher named Fabiola.

◀ Jaime was a tough, but good teacher.

A Move to the United States

Jaime was a great teacher. But teachers in Bolivia were not paid well. Jaime and Fabiola decided to move to the United States. They thought that things would be better for their family there. In 1963, Jaime and his family arrived in Pasadena, California. Jaime went back to school to learn to speak English. Even though he had taught for over nine years in Bolivia, he needed to go to college again to learn how to be a teacher in the United States. While he went to school, he had many jobs and worked very hard.

Jaime, Fabiola, and their son moved to the city of Pasadena, California. ▶

A Teacher Again

Ten years later, at the age of 43, Jaime became a teacher again. In 1974, he started teaching at Garfield High School. His first few weeks were hard. The students did not listen to him. Sometimes they didn't even come to class. He thought about quitting. But then he decided he would make it work. He told the students that they needed *ganas* (GAH-nas). This is the Spanish word for having a desire, in this case a desire to **succeed** (suk-SEED). Jaime told them that once they had *ganas*, learning would be easy. The students began to listen to Jaime.

Jaime was able to get his students to want to learn.

Making Math Fun

Jaime learned about an exam in a kind of math called **calculus** (KAL-kyoo-lus). Students who did well on the exam could earn **credits** (KRED-its) for college. Calculus is hard to learn, and Garfield did not have any classes in it. So Jaime started one. In 1981, Jaime became the head of the math department at Garfield. The next year, eighteen of his students took the calculus exam, and all of them passed. Some people thought Jaime's students had **cheated** (CHEE-ted). But the students took the test again and passed again. Jaime and his students showed everyone that they could learn anything they wanted to.

Edward James Olmos played Jaime in a movie called *Stand and Deliver*, which was about Jaime's success at Garfield. ▶

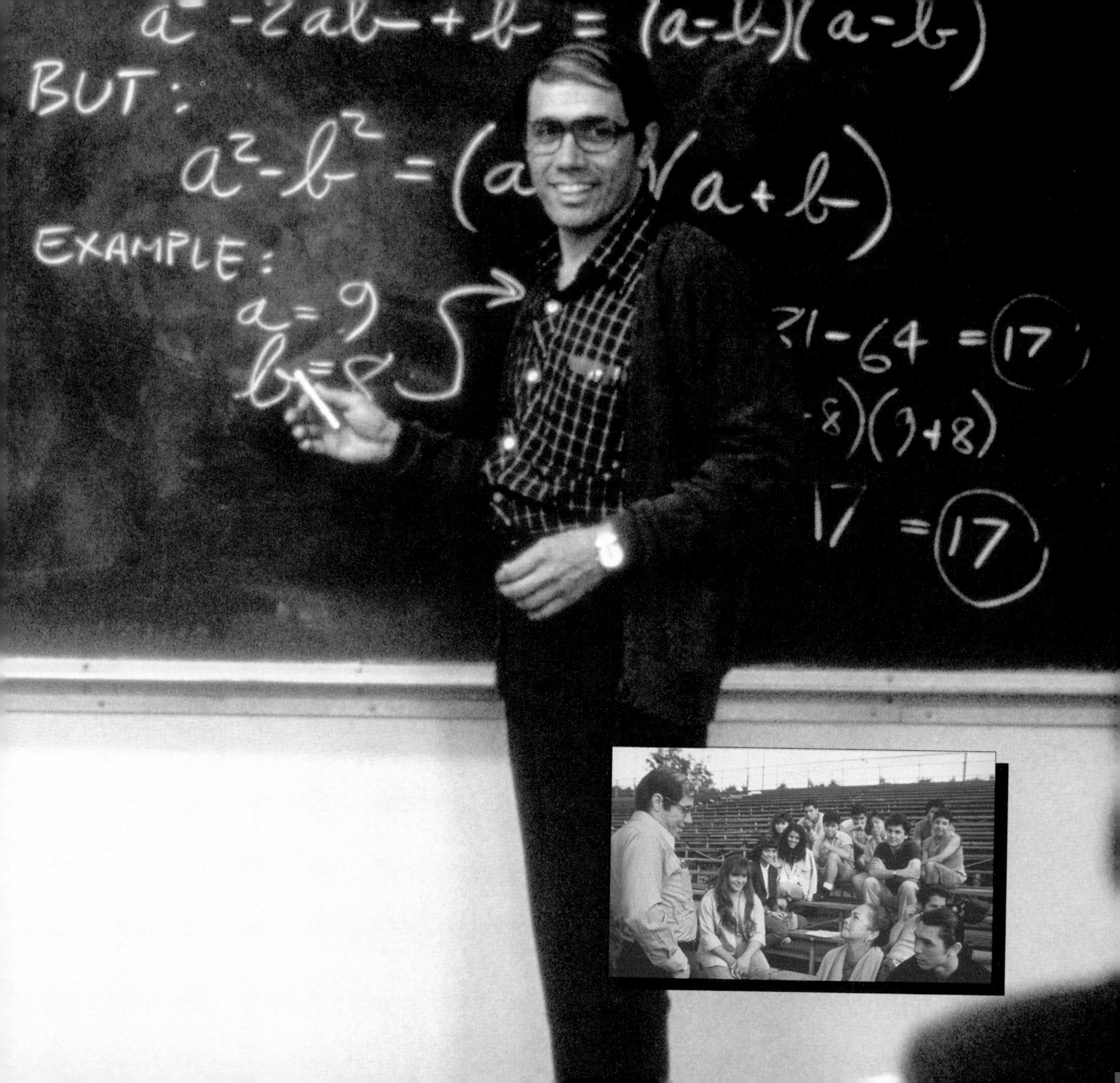
BUT:
EXAMPLE:
a = 9
b = 8
= 17
17 = 17

New Projects

Many people admired the way Jaime had **inspired** (in-SPYRD) his students to learn calculus. In 1988, a movie called *Stand and Deliver* was made about Jaime. In 1991, Jaime decided to teach at a different school, Hiram Johnson High School. He started a calculus program there too. He began a summer program where students could visit jobs and see how often math is used. Jaime also made videos and TV shows about such jobs. Jaime started another project in which people talk to students about the ways in which they use math.

◄ Presidents Ronald Reagan and George Bush praised Jaime for his accomplishments.

All You Need Is Ganas

Today, Jaime looks for more ways to get students interested in science and math. He has won many awards. It is important to Jaime that he helps students get ready for their future.

When Jaime speaks to students, he always tells them that they can be whatever they want to be. Each person has to decide if he or she wants to be a winner or a loser. Jaime believes that you make your own successes in life. All you need is to have *ganas* and to believe in your dreams.

Glossary

calculus (KAL-kyoo-lus) The study of ways to get answers in math.

cheat (CHEET) To act in an unfair or dishonest way.

credit (KRED-it) A point that you earn for taking an exam or a class that can be used toward finishing college.

electrical engineer (ee-LEK-trih-kul en-jin-EER) A person who studies how electricity can be used to make or do things.

electricity (el-ek-TRIH-sih-tee) A form of energy that can produce light, heat, or motion.

experiment (ex-PEER-ih-ment) To carry out tests that let you find out something you want to know.

ganas (GAH-nas) Spanish for "having a desire."

inspire (in-SPYR) To fill with a wish to do or say something.

physics (FIZ-iks) The science of how things move and how work is done.

strategy (STRA-tuh-jee) A careful plan.

succeed (suk-SEED) To do what you plan to do.

Index